DEC

W9-CNF-933

WITHDRAWN

Your Research Paper

by Ann Graham Gaines

Enslow Elementary

an imprint of

Enslow Publishers, Inc.

40 Industrial Road
Box 398
Berkeley Heights, NJ 07922
USA

http://www.enslow.com

Enslow Elementary, an imprint of Enslow Publishers, Inc.

Enslow Elementary® is a registered trademark of Enslow Publishers, Inc.

Copyright © 2009 by Enslow Publishers, Inc.

All rights reserved.

No part of this book may be reproduced by any means without the
written permission of the publisher.

Library of Congress Cataloging-in-Publication Data
Gaines, Ann.
    Ace your research paper / Ann Graham Gaines.
        p. cm. — (Ace it! information literacy series)
    Includes bibliographical references and index.
    Summary: "Readers will learn how to research, take notes, write, and revise their research
papers"—Provided by publisher.
    ISBN-13: 978-0-7660-3390-0
    ISBN-10: 0-7660-3390-2
    1. Report writing—Study and teaching (Elementary)—United States. 2. English language—
Composition and exercises—Study and teaching (Elementary) 3. Research—United States.
I. Title.
    LB1047.3.G35 2009
    372.13'0281—dc22
                                    2008024884

Printed in the United States of America

10 9 8 7 6 5 4 3 2 1

To Our Readers:
We have done our best to make sure all Internet Addresses in this book were active and
appropriate when we went to press. However, the author and the publisher have no control over
and assume no liability for the material available on those Internet sites or on other Web sites
they may link to. Any comments or suggestions can be sent by e-mail to comments@enslow.com
or to the address on the back cover.

♻ Enslow Publishers, Inc., is committed to printing our books on recycled paper. The paper
in every book contains 10% to 30% post-consumer waste (PCW). The cover board on the outside
of each book contains 100% PCW. Our goal is to do our part to help young people and the
environment too!

Cover photos: iStockphoto.com/Sean Locke; iStockphoto.com/Marilyn Nieves (background image).
Interior photos: Associated Press Images/Phil Sandlin, p. 14; BigStockPhoto.com/Marmion, p. 25;
Corbis/Fancy/Veer, p. 7; Corbis/LWA-Sharie Kennedy, p. 42; Ellen B. Senisi, p. 36; Getty Images/Thomas
Barwick, p. 18; The Image Works/Margot Granitsas, p. 32; iStockphoto.com/Johnny Scriv, p. 12;
iStockphoto.com/Jacek Chabraszewski, p. 19; iStockphoto.com/Christine Balderas, p. 30 (top and
bottom); iStockphoto.com/Andres Peiro, p. 3, 5, 9, 13, 17, 31, 35, 37, 41; iStockphoto.com/Mustafa
Deliormanli, p. 43; Jupiter Images/Tanya Constantine/Blend Images, p. 8; Photo Edit/Myrleen Ferguson
Cate, p. 39; Photolibrary.com, pp. 4, 11.

Contents

Teachers know that writing research papers will help you succeed in life.

What Is a Research Paper, Anyway?

What is a research paper, anyway? That's a great question. The first thing to know is the meaning of the word *research*. To do research is to hunt for information about a topic. A topic is one general idea. For example, your topic could be brown bears, Miley Cyrus, or the Grand Canyon. When you collect information, organize it, and write about it, you are writing a research paper.

Kids mostly write research papers for school. You could also do research for a scout project, an online magazine, or just for fun. You might even turn your research paper into a different kind of presentation, like a poster or an oral report.

Why do teachers ask students to write research papers? They know it will help you succeed in life. Doing research teaches you how to find and present information.

Teacher Jack Wilde from New Hampshire says he likes students to write research papers because it helps them become "independent learners."[1] Independent learners can find information by themselves and learn about the things that interest them. A teacher from the state of Washington, Steve Freeman, thinks research helps students become good at problem solving.[2]

The first time you are assigned a research paper, you might feel nervous. The project might seem like a lot of work. You might worry that you don't know what to do. Relax. This book will give you clear, step-by-step instructions to get the job done.

The first four steps of the research paper process are called prewriting. The prefix *pre-* means "before," so

Steps for Writing a Research Paper

Step 1: Understand Your Assignment

Step 2: Choose Your Topic

Step 3: Research

Step 4: Make an Outline

Step 5: Draft and Revise Your Paper

Step 6: Peer Review and Publication

prewriting means "before writing." This is what you do when you are planning your final product. Imagine that you are making a salad. Before you create the salad, you need to gather your ingredients and chop them up. Prewriting is gathering and preparing the ingredients of your research paper.

Now it's time to get started!

Don't worry too much about your research paper. This book gives you easy-to-follow steps!

As soon as your teacher hands out your assignment, start getting organized!

First Things First: Understand Your Assignment

Before you begin writing, start with **Step 1: Understand your assignment**. Maybe your teacher wants you to write about animals. Or, for your scout badge in astronomy, you have to write a big research paper about space. Maybe you've entered your newspaper's Martin Luther King, Jr. Day essay contest.

Step 1: Understand Your Assignment

Step 2: Choose Your Topic

Step 3: Research

Step 4: Make an Outline

Step 5: Draft and Revise Your Paper

Step 6: Peer Review and Publication

It's also important to find out what kind of research you need to do. Your teacher might ask you to use a book, an encyclopedia, and a magazine article. Find out what your paper should look like. Should it have five paragraphs, or does it have to fill two pages? Do you have to type your paper on a computer? Do you need to include a title page, a bibliography, or illustrations?

Some teachers will give you a useful tool called a rubric. This is a chart that your teacher will use to grade your paper. The chart lists all the requirements for your paper—things like a clear topic, excellent research, good organization, colorful illustrations, and so on. Your rubric is your guide to creating exactly what your teacher has assigned you. If you get a rubric, use it to understand your assignment. Keep it by your side every step of the way.

Do not leave **Step 1** until you know your due date! Write it down on your calendar. Ask someone to remind you when the date gets close. Then make a timeline for your work. This will help you keep track of what needs to happen when. First, figure out how many days or weeks you have to finish your assignment. Cross out days when you won't be able to work on your project. For a big project like a research paper, you need to break your work down into a series of small steps.

Use a calendar to keep track of important steps for your research paper.

Here is how you should divide up the time you have for doing your paper:

10% brainstorming
25% researching and taking notes
20% making your outline
25% drafting your paper
20% revising, editing, and finishing your paper[3]

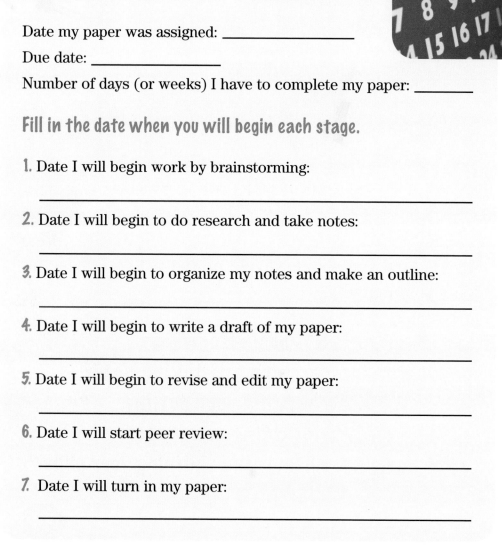

[You can copy this timeline onto another piece of paper to create your own. Do not write in this book!]

Research Paper Timeline

As soon as you get your assignment, make a timeline that says what you're going to do when.

Date my paper was assigned: _____

Due date: _____

Number of days (or weeks) I have to complete my paper: _____

Fill in the date when you will begin each stage.

1. Date I will begin work by brainstorming:

_____

2. Date I will begin to do research and take notes:

_____

3. Date I will begin to organize my notes and make an outline:

_____

4. Date I will begin to write a draft of my paper:

_____

5. Date I will begin to revise and edit my paper:

_____

6. Date I will start peer review:

_____

7. Date I will turn in my paper:

_____

Finding Focus: Choose Your Topic

Now that you understand your assignment, you are ready for **Step 2: Choose Your Topic**. If you're assigned to write about animals, you know your general topic. Now you have to get more specific. You need to choose what kind of animal you want to write about. If you don't get specific, you'll end up with a very large topic. You'll gather too much information. Your paper will be too long and too hard to organize.

You might want to focus on unusual animals. That topic is still too big. Think smaller. Try to think of just one unusual animal you want to learn about. Now is the

Step 1: Understand Your Assignment

Step 2: Choose Your Topic

Step 3: Research

Step 4: Make an Outline

Step 5: Draft and Revise Your Paper

Step 6: Peer Review and Publication

The armadillo is a great topic for a research paper about unusual animals.

time for brainstorming. Make a list of all the ideas that come into your head. Still stuck? Do a little reading. You could browse in an encyclopedia or a big book about animals. Maybe you'll become interested in animals with unusual ways of defending themselves. Now, narrow your topic even more. Finally, you might decide to write about the amazing armadillo. This animal has a shell that works like armor.

Next, ask yourself questions about the topic you have chosen. Some teachers suggest asking yourself, "What do I want to know more about?"[4] Maybe you wonder why armadillos need to defend themselves. You might want to know more about the animals that attack them.

Caution! Make sure your topic isn't too small. A topic that's too specific is as bad as a topic that's too general. For example, let's say you choose the topic of where armadillos live. You won't find enough information to make a good paper. Your paper will be too short!

Topics That Won't Work

Look for a topic that's not too big or too small. Make sure it's interesting and matches your assignment, too! Here are some topics that won't make a good research paper.

1. **American animals:** There are too many American animals. Your paper would take forever to write!

2. **What bison eat:** Since buffalo only eat grass, this topic is way too small.

3. **Big brown bats in winter:** These animals hibernate during the winter, so this paper would be pretty boring!

DANGER: Procrastination!

Do you procrastinate? That means putting work off until the last minute. If you wait too long to start work on a project, you can't do a good job. Experts give these tips to procrastinators:

- Block off time to work on your project. On your calendar, look for time when you will be free to work. Decide how many hours you'll work on those days.

- Sit by yourself when you work on a writing project. It will be hard to work if you have friends or family around. Try to find a quiet place where you can work alone.

- Avoid distractions. Turn off the television or your MP3 player while you work. If you have a cell phone, do not answer it unless it is your parents or an actual emergency.

- Expect the unexpected! Put aside extra time, just in case your family's plans change. Let's say your mom can't take you to the library on Thursday night. Saturday afternoon could be your backup plan.

- If you start worrying that you'll never finish, break down your project into small steps. This will make it easier, and will help you feel calmer.[5]

Think Like a Detective: Research

Once you choose your topic, you're ready to begin **Step 3: Research**. One college professor tells his students that when they do research, they should think of themselves as detectives who are collecting evidence.[6]

First, think about where to find sources. Sources provide information. In the old days, most sources were printed—they were books, magazines, or newspapers. Today we have electronic sources, too, like Web sites and databases. There are even more types of sources. For example, if you need information about the civil rights movement, your own

Step 1: Understand Your Assignment

Step 2: Choose Your Topic

Step 3: Research

Step 4: Make an Outline

Step 5: Draft and Revise Your Paper

Step 6: Peer Review and Publication

Your library's catalog is a great place to start your research.

grandmother could be a source of information. You could ask her what it was like to live during that time in history.

Sometimes you can find sources for your research at home. You could look up information on your computer or in your own books. The best place to do research, though, is your school or public library.

At the library, start by using the catalog. Today almost all libraries have their catalogs on computers. Before you use the catalog, think of some keywords related to your topic. They will help you find useful sources. For a paper about an armadillo, you might use keywords such as *armadillo*, *desert*, *armor*, and *defenses*.

Type your keywords into the library catalog's search box. Press ENTER. The computer will show you a list of sources about your keywords. For a book, you will see its title and call number. This number tells a librarian where to put the book on the library shelf. You can use it to find the book. To find magazine articles, ask a librarian to help you use the *Readers' Guide to Periodical Literature* or special magazine databases. As you explore the library, remember that librarians are expert detectives. They will help you learn how to use the library. They will also guide you to the materials you need.

As you conduct your research, keep thinking like a detective. Look for clues that lead you to useful information. The first books you find might not have what you want.

Good researchers think like detectives.

They might be too simple or too hard to read. One way to find just the right sources is to browse. That means to look through the shelves until something catches your eye. When you find a book by its call number, look at other books nearby. They might help you, too!

Browse *inside* sources, too. You do not need to read every word at first. Flip through a book or magazine article to see if it has helpful information or interesting illustrations. Remember, a picture or map can provide just as much information as words can.

The Internet can also be a useful source. To get started, look at your list of keywords. At a computer with Internet access, type in the name of a search engine. This is a Web site that provides sources of information. Google.com and AskKids.com are good search engines. Type your keywords into the search box, and press ENTER. You will see a results page—a list of Web sites that include your keywords. Click on a link—an underlined word or phrase—to visit the site. Scan the Web site for useful information. Once you're done with that one, go back to your results page and look at other sites.

Both Web sites and printed sources often provide clues that lead you to other sources. In printed sources, flip to the end and look for a Further Reading list or bibliography. Many Web sites contain links to other helpful sites.

As you find some sources, you may want to begin taking notes. Look for information that answers the questions you have about your topic. If you are lucky, you will find many good sources. Soon you will have to choose exactly which ones to use. To do so, you'll need to evaluate the sources. That means you'll decide whether they really are good sources to use for your research project.

A good source is relevant. That means it is closely related to your topic. If you're writing about armadillos in Texas, an article about armadillos in South America isn't relevant to your topic. One good way to find out if a book is relevant is to look at its table of contents. The table of contents is at the front of a book. It tells you the number of chapters, the

Spider Map

Write your research topic inside the circle. Write the questions you want to answer on the legs. As your research leads you to the answers, you can write them on the straight lines. This map will help when it is time to write your paper.

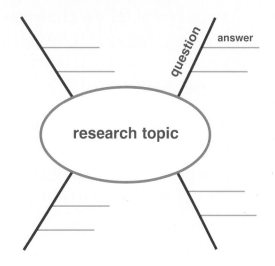

question   answer

research topic

21

Online Safety

The Internet is a great place to find information. After all, surfing the Web is tons of fun. Unfortunately, it can also be dangerous. If you find a Web site that makes you uncomfortable, leave!

When you're online, you might be asked to register for a Web site or to become a member of a group. Ask a trusted adult before you follow the instructions. You must never give out personal information unless a parent or teacher says it's okay. Personal information includes things like your name, address, phone number, e-mail address, and the name of your school.

Never send a photograph of yourself to a Web site. Do not respond to mean messages. If someone you talk to online wants to meet you in person, do not reply. Show the message to a trusted adult. They'll let you know if it's okay to write back.[7]

titles of the chapters, and what page each chapter starts on. Look at the table of contents for important clues about how a book is organized.

You can also go to the very back of a book to find the index. That's an alphabetical list of the topics inside a book. The index tells you what pages to turn to for information about each topic. To use an index, look for your keywords in the alphabetical list.

As you evaluate a source, decide whether its information is factual—based on the truth. You should not use a work of fiction to write a research paper. Also, beware—the author of your source may sometimes state opinions rather than facts. You can include both facts and opinions in your research paper, but make sure you know which is which. For example, no one could really argue with the fact that your sneakers are red. But they might disagree with your opinion that red is the best color for all sneakers! Finally, check to make sure your source is up to date. Old sources can lose their accuracy fast![8]

It's really important to evaluate Web sites. Keep in mind that they are not always reliable. After all, absolutely anyone can post information on the Internet. Usually, the best Web sites are created by experts. To find out who created a Web site, try looking at the bottom of the home page or click on a link called Contact Us. In one of those places, you often see the name of a person (like scientist Stephen Hawking) or an organization (like Drexel University). If you see a university, school, or museum, that's an excellent sign that you have found a good Web site.

Once you have decided which sources to use, you need to take detailed notes. Good notes help you remember the information you find. They also help you organize your

The Tail End of a Web Site

Web site addresses end with two or three letters that come after a period, or dot. This ending is called a domain extension. Extensions tell you what type of Web site you are visiting. Here's a guide to some common domain extensions. Notice that two-letter extensions stand for countries outside of the United States.

.com   commercial: used by businesses and companies

.edu   education: used by schools such as public schools, colleges, and universities

.gov   government: used by town, city, state, and national governments

.org   organization: used by churches and charitable institutions

.ca   Canada

.ru   Russia

.uk   United Kingdom

information, and tell you where you found it. Notes are very important later, too, when it is time to create a bibliography for your paper.

People have different ways of taking notes. Some write by hand on lined note cards. Some use a notebook.

Others like to take notes by typing them on a computer. Your teacher might tell you which way to take notes. Otherwise, choose the method you like most.

People also differ in *when* they take notes. You can take notes as you read. Another way is to read through a chapter or article and then go back to take notes. Again, experiment with several ways and choose what works best for you.

When you take notes, you usually should not copy down complete sentences. Write only a few words to remind you about a fact or idea. Rephrase the author's words. That means to write them in a different way, using your own words.

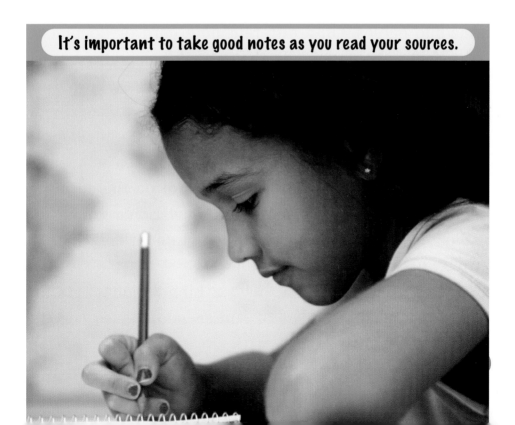

It's important to take good notes as you read your sources.

Sometimes you will find a sentence that you really like. For example, a *Ranger Rick* magazine article describes the armadillo as a "hopping armored tank."[9] Maybe you want to quote these exact words in your paper. To quote means to copy someone else's words. When you quote an author in a research paper, you must tell your reader who wrote or spoke the words. In your notes, mark these words with quotation marks (" "). If you copy someone's words without telling your readers what you're doing, you plagiarize. If you plagiarize, you are cheating.

It is a good idea to label your notes with a topic. For example, on one note card—or in one section of a computer document—you could record facts about armadillo babies. On a different note card or document, write facts about animals that attack armadillos. Mark your notes with subject headings such as BABIES or WHAT EATS ARMADILLOS.

Along with your note for each fact or quote, identify the source where you found it. Since you'll also be keeping a separate list of all your sources (more on this in just a minute), you could just use an abbreviation such as the author's last name or a short version of the title. Be sure to also write down the page number.

Research papers end with a bibliography, or a list of sources used. This list of source notes gives specific information about each source you used, such as the author name, book title, and page number. There are different ways to write a bibliography. Your teacher or librarian can help you decide on the right way, if your assignment did not include specific instructions. Also see the graphic organizer on page 28 and the information about creating a bibliography on pages 42–43.

Avoiding Plagiarism

Plagiarism happens when you do not write your paper all by yourself. Instead, you use other people's words without saying so. That can happen if you're not very careful when you take notes. Never copy exact sentences from a source unless you see something that you really want to quote. If you do quote someone else's words, use quotation marks (" ") around the words. Write the name of the person who said them. Include the source in your bibliography.

Teachers see plagiarism as a very serious problem. If they believe students have plagiarized, they often give students a failing grade. When you reach high school and college, plagiarism can get you kicked out of school. If you want help making sure you haven't plagiarized by accident, ask your teacher or a librarian.

Source Notes for My Bibliography

For a book:

Author(s) (last name, then first name): _____

Title: _____

Copyright date (find this on the copyright page): _____

Name of publisher (from the copyright page): _____

For a magazine article:

Author(s) (last name, then first name): _____

Article title: _____

Magazine title: _____

Date article was published: _____

Page numbers: _____

For an Internet article:

Author or organization's name (if you can find it): _____

Name of the Web page: _____

URL (the Web page address): _____

Date you first looked at the article: _____

For an encyclopedia article:

Name of the article (entry name): _____

Title of the encyclopedia: _____

Copyright date: _____

After you take notes, sort them. Put them into an order that makes sense. For example, you might want to group information about armadillo claws with armadillo burrows, since armadillos use their claws to dig their burrows. As you look at your notes and sort them, you might come up with new questions about your topic. If that happens, do a bit more research and find the answers.

Now is also a good time to reach some conclusions about your topic. You draw conclusions when you put together clues to figure out something new. For example, if you read that armadillos need low trees and brush to hide in, you might conclude that armadillos cannot live in an area with no plants. Your conclusion is what you want your reader to remember about your research paper.

In a book called *The Life of Mammals*, author David Attenborough writes an entire chapter about animals that eat insects. He talks about insect eaters that have special protection, including the armored armadillo. Below you will see part of what Attenborough wrote. Then you will see two index cards with a student's notes.

The biggest armadillo alive today is about the size of a large bulldog. It [digs] huge tunnels into the base of termite hills. It can dig much faster than you can. This giant, unlike the rest of its family, eats very little other than insects. It specializes in insects that can be collected by the hundred [such as] ants and termites.

Collecting such insects as these requires special equipment. First you must be [a] powerful digger to be able to rip apart termite hills. . . . And second, you have to have an efficient way of gathering up insects in bulk. The giant armadillo . . . has more teeth than almost any other mammal—about a hundred.[10]

> The biggest armadillo alive today is about the size of a large bulldog. It can dig faster than you can and makes tunnels.
>
> Since it is so big, it only eats insects that can be found in large numbers. Likes termites and ants. It has about a hundred teeth.

What's wrong with this index card? It doesn't have a clear subject. There are too many different pieces of information. There's also a direct quote that isn't marked, "The biggest armadillo alive today is about the size of a large bulldog." And there's no source at the bottom!

> Giant Armadillo — Food
> Insects by the hundred
> Likes ants and termites
>
> Good at digging for food
> Lots of teeth
>
> Attenborough, The Life of Mammals, pg. 56.

What's great about this note card? It has a subject. It lists information from the source in the student's own words. And it identifies the source.

Get Organized: Make an Outline

You've done your research, and you're bursting with exciting information for your research paper. Is it time to start writing yet? Not quite! You'll have a much easier time if you organize your paper first. Decide on a main idea for each paragraph. You will identify each main idea in a topic sentence. Then you'll add details to fill out each paragraph.

There's more than one way to get your ideas in order. One way is to use an outline. Another is to use a mind map. A third way is to lay out your note cards so

Step 1: Understand Your Assignment

Step 2: Choose Your Topic

Step 3: Research

Step 4: Make an Outline

Step 5: Draft and Revise Your Paper

Step 6: Peer Review and Publication

31

You've taken lots of notes. Now it's time to organize all that information!

that the information tells your story. Whichever method you use, it will help you get organized and give you a plan.

An outline is an organizer. You use numbers and letters to put information in ordered groups. You can see an example of an outline on the next page.

When you use a mind map, you organize your information in a visual way. Write your topic in a circle in the center of a piece of paper. Surround that circle with other circles, and write your main ideas. Add details on branches connected to your main idea circles.

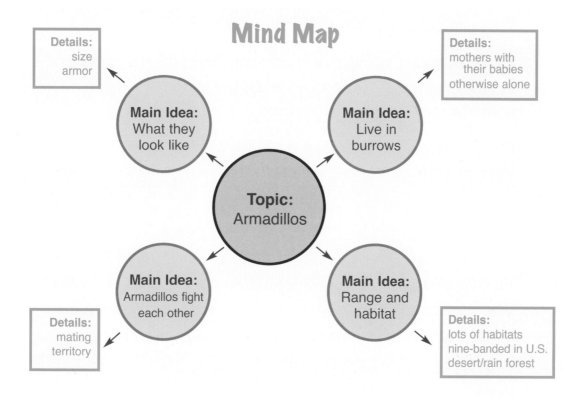

Mind Map

Details:
size
armor

Main Idea:
What they
look like

Details:
mothers with
their babies
otherwise alone

Main Idea:
Live in
burrows

Topic:
Armadillos

Main Idea:
Armadillos fight
each other

Main Idea:
Range and
habitat

Details:
mating
territory

Details:
lots of habitats
nine-banded in U.S.
desert/rain forest

As you work on your outline or mindmap, you might discover that some of your information doesn't belong. That's okay. Just don't use it. On the other hand, you might discover that you have some new questions. Then you need to do more research. Take time to fill in your gaps.

The Beginning and the End

Research papers start with an introduction. It says what your paper is about. Think about how to get your reader interested. You could begin with a question or a fun fact.

Research papers end with a conclusion. That's where you sum up what you know. Think about what you want your reader to remember. Make sure it is exciting!

Introductions and conclusions can be hard to write. You might want to write them after you've written the rest of your paper.

In your outline or mind map, you can include more than just main ideas and details. For example, show where you want to add quotations, maps, charts, or photographs.

You can use an outline like the one on the opposite page to plan your research paper.

A Good Armadillo Outline

I. Introduction ········· (absolutely necessary!)

II. What do they look like? (the writer chooses specific details)
   A. Size
      1. Largest is giant armadillo
      2. Can become very large and heavy
   B. Armor
      1. Heavy armor plates on back
      2. Soft, hairy skin on bellies

III. Range and habitat
   A. All kinds—North and South ······ (good—outlines aren't written in complete sentences)
      America (include map here)
   B. Only nine-banded armadillo lives in U.S.

IV. Live in burrows
   A. Mothers live with their babies
   B. Otherwise alone

V. Armadillos can fight each other!
   A. Mating
   B. Territory

VI. Conclusion: armadillo range is expanding,
   so you might see one in your town!

Your outline is ready. Now it's time to write, write, write!

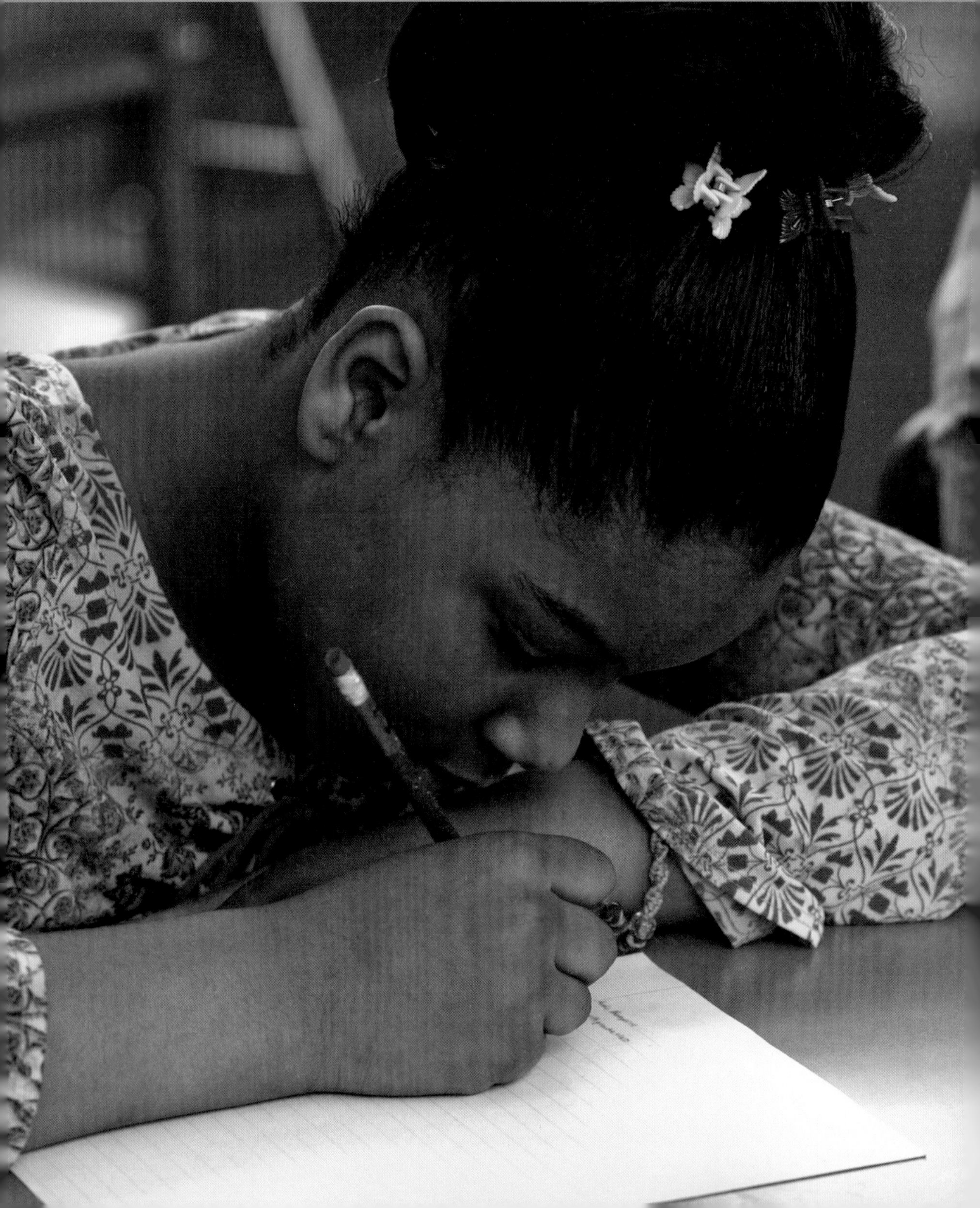

Ready, Set, Write! Draft and Revise Your Paper

Finally, you have reached **Step 5: Draft and Revise Your Paper**. A draft is a first version—a try. It can be tricky to get started. If words don't come to you right away, reread your notes. As you write, follow your outline or mind map. Remember to give every paragraph a topic sentence telling its main idea. Then add details.

When you draft, don't worry about making every sentence perfect. You will do that soon enough. As you draft, mark words you're not sure how to spell, or facts you want to check. You can use a pen, a sticky note, a highlighter, or a bracketed note [like this one].

Step 1: Understand Your Assignment

Step 2: Choose Your Topic

Step 3: Research

Step 4: Make an Outline

Step 5: Draft and Revise Your Paper

Step 6: Peer Review and Publication

Once you're done with your draft, you're ready to revise and edit your paper. This is your chance to improve your paper. But you don't have to change everything. Revision is like polishing the rough parts of the paper.

Before you begin to revise, it's a good idea to review your instructions. If your teacher gave you a rubric, look at it. Make sure that your paper matches the assignment.

Next, look at your draft. Read it aloud. This will help you find out if your words make sense. Mark changes you want to make with a colored pencil or highlighter, or use the highlight feature in your word processing program. You might decide to rewrite sentences or move some around.

This is your chance to make your paper exciting. Cut parts that do not connect to your main ideas. Take out boring facts. Also, think about your word choice. Make sure you aren't using the same word over and over again.

Paragraph Sketch

Write your main idea in the large box. Write details that support the main idea in the smaller boxes. If a detail does not support the main idea, leave it out!

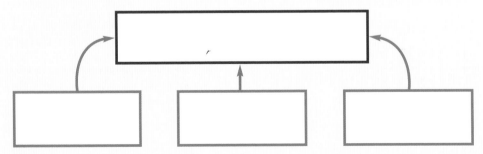

Overcoming Writer's Block

"Writer's block" describes the frustrating feeling of being unable to write. You might get writer's block if you don't understand what to do, if you haven't done enough research, or if you find your paper boring. To get over writer's block, review the assignment. Dig up more exciting details. Then focus on one paragraph—or even just one sentence—at a time.[11]

Try asking your teacher or another adult to look at your draft. Then you can see if you're on the right track. It can also help just to talk about your topic with a friend or family member. This can help make you feel more confident about how much you have learned, and how much you have to say.

When you are done marking changes you want to make, either neatly rewrite your paper by hand or go back onto the computer to fix it. Don't forget to save your new work if you are using a computer!

Next, proofread your paper. That means checking your capitalization, spelling, and punctuation. If you aren't sure where your errors are, check a dictionary, thesaurus, or grammar book. You can also ask your teacher for help. Now is another good time to review your assignment and rubric.

Here is an example of a student's revised paper. The parts in red show how much she changed.

The Armored Armadillo

What is the only mammal that lives in a suit of armor? The armadillo! This clawed animal is covered in bony plates. When it rolls up into a ball, all of its weak spots disappear and no predators can eat it.

All armadillos have that armor. But they don't all look alike. For one thing, they come in different sizes. The giant armadillo grows up to about 40 inches long. Others are about 30 inches from the tip of their nose to the end of their tail. Armadillos are brown or gray. An armadillo's plates cover its tail, the top of its head, and its back, shoulders, and hips. It also has some soft, hairy skin.

Scientists think there are about twenty different species of armadillos. They all live in North and South America. Only one species lives in the United States. It is the nine-banded armadillo. There are a lot of armadillos in Texas.

Wherever they live, armadillos use their claws to dig dens or burrows lined with grass. Armadillos usually live alone, but babies live together with their mother. Armadillos usually have four babies at one time.

Armadillos are not peaceful animals! They sometimes fight over mates and territory. They kick at each other and squeal.

Armadillos seem unusual to many Americans. Many people never see them, except maybe at the zoo. That is probably going to change. The nine-banded armadillo is moving to new places all the time. Maybe an armadillo will show up in your state!

Chapter

6

The Finish Line: Peer Review and Publication

The finish line is in sight! We've reached **Step 6: Peer Review and Publication**. In a peer review, you ask a friend or classmate to read your paper. Ask your partner to tell you how you could make your paper better. Try not to get upset if she points out a place where you made a mistake. After all, that's what peer review is for. It is better to find out now than to get a lower grade on your paper!

When it's your turn to give a peer review, think before you speak. Point out parts you don't understand. Be careful to talk about the

Step 1: Understand Your Assignment

Step 2: Choose Your Topic

Step 3: Research

Step 4: Make an Outline

Step 5: Draft and Revise Your Paper

Step 6: Peer Review and Publication

41

writing and not the person who wrote it. Be specific. Don't say, "You did a bad job here." Instead, say something like "This section is confusing. I don't understand what a bony plate is." Don't go overboard when you criticize. Also, it's very important to remember to praise the writer! Talk about the parts you find easy to read or exciting.[12]

After you've gotten your peer review, make some final changes. Then it's time to think about how your finished paper will look. Make sure it is neat and you have at least 1-inch margins around the edges of each piece of paper.

Next, add your extras. First, create your title page. It should include your name, the title of your paper, and the class you're in (or the contest you're entering). Your bibliography goes on its own page. Arrange your sources in an alphabetical list by the authors' last names. You can also add illustrations, maps, or charts to your paper. If you've drawn your own illustrations, sign your name. If you've copied them from somewhere else, write the name of the source below the illustration.

Do you want your research paper to be *really* good? Find a partner and try a peer review.

42

An Armadillo Bibliography

Jango-Cohen, Judith. *Armadillos.* New York: Benchmark Books, 2004.

Library of Congress. "How High Can a Nine-banded Armadillo Jump?" *Everyday Mysteries.* 8 April 2008. <http://www.loc.gov/rr/scitech/mysteries/armadillo.html>.

McDonough, C.M. and Loughry, W.J. "Armadillos." *Grzimek's Animal Life Encyclopedia.* Farmington Hills, Mich.: Gale Cengage, 2003, Vol. 13, pp. 181–192.

Mealy, Nora Steiner. "Here Come the Armadillos!" *Ranger Rick.* November 1, 2000: 3.

Once you've finished your paper, you might want to do more than just turn it in. You could send it to your school newspaper or an online magazine. You might be able to turn it into a display for the wall in your classroom or the exhibit case at your library.

Once you're all done, it's time for evaluation. If you've written your paper for school, your teacher will give it a grade. Have a conference with your teacher to find out what he or she liked about it—and what you could have done better. It's a great idea to think about how you think the project went, too. You can use an evaluation form like the one at the end of this chapter to reflect on your own work.

Evaluate yourself honestly each time you do a research paper. Then your research and writing skills will improve every time. This will be a wonderful reason to celebrate!

[Copy onto a separate piece of paper.]

Evaluate Yourself!

Self-evaluation can help you figure out what went right and wrong with your research paper. You can use this form every time you do a research project.

About my report on _____

Circle the phrase that describes how you did on your report, in your own opinion:

I followed the instructions.	Great	OK	Hard for me
I used my time well.	Great	OK	Hard for me
I found good sources for my paper.	Great	OK	Hard for me
I used different kinds of sources.	Great	OK	Hard for me
My sources were up to date.	Great	OK	Hard for me

Answering the following questions might help you next time:

How did I find my best sources? _____

_____

What did I do best on this project? (for example, research or

  illustrations) _____

What did I want to learn from this project? _____

What did I learn? _____

What will I do differently next time? _____

_____

Glossary

bibliography—A list of sources used in a piece of writing.

brainstorm—To come up with ideas and write them down as they pop into your head.

browse—To look through something quickly without reading every word.

call number—A number that tells where a book should go on the library shelf.

catalog—A collection of cards or a computer database that lists everything a library holds.

conclusion—A statement that sums up or makes a judgment about something.

copyright page—The page in a book that says who published it, where, and when. It is usually near the front of the book.

draft—To write the first version of a paper.

evaluate—To decide if something is good or bad.

evidence—Facts that prove a statement or support a main idea.

fiction—Writing that tells a made-up story.

home page—A Web site's main page.

index—An alphabetical list of topics inside a book.

keywords—Words or phrases used to search for information.

margins—Blank spaces around the edges of a piece of paper.

oral report—A speech that gives an audience information about a certain topic.

plagiarize—To take someone else's work without giving credit. Instead, you say it is your own.

prewriting—Preparing and organizing before drafting a paper.

proofread—To check writing for mistakes in grammar, punctuation, and spelling.

quote—To use someone else's exact words.

relevant—Directly related to a certain topic.

reliable—Dependable and accurate.

rephrase—To say something in a different way, in your own words.

research—To search for information about a particular topic.

rubric—A chart that tells what a piece of writing should include.

search engine—A Web site that helps you search for information on other Web sites.

sources—Books, newspapers, Web sites, and other places to find information.

table of contents—The list of chapter titles and page numbers in the front of a book or other publication.

topic—Subject, or main idea; what you are writing, reading, or speaking about.

topic sentence—The sentence that tells the topic of a paragraph.

URL—A Web site address, usually beginning with *http://* or *www.*

Further Reading

Books

Jarnow, Jill. *Writing to Explain.* New York: PowerKids Press, 2006.

Rau, Dana Meachen. *Ace Your Writing Assignment.* Berkeley Heights, N.J.: Enslow Publishers, 2009.

Somervill, Barbara A. *Written Reports.* Chicago: Heinemann Library, 2008.

On the Internet

How to Write a Research Paper
http://www.infoplease.com/homework/t1termpaper1.html

Tips for Writing Essays
http://www.factmonster.com/homework/hwessays.html

Write a Winning Research Report
http://content.scholastic.com/browse/article.jsp?id=1610

Chapter Notes

1. Jack Wilde, *A Door Opens: Writing in Fifth Grade* (Portsmouth, NH: Heinemann, 1993), p. 72.

2. William J. Valmont, "What Do Teachers Do in Technology-Rich Classrooms?" *Linking Literacy and Technology* (Newark, Del.: International Reading Association, 2000), p. 191.

3. Amy J.K. Borrell, "Write a Winning Research Report," *Scholastic Kids*, n.d., <http://content.scholastic.com/browse/article.jsp?id=1610> (February 17, 2008).

4. El Paso Collaborative for Academic Excellence, "Third Grade Informational Text Writing," 2003, <http://epcae.org/literacy/curriculum/informational/InfoThird.pdf> (February 17, 2008).

5. "Tips from an Ex-Procrastinator," *Scholastic Kids*, n.d., <http://content.scholastic.com/browse/article.jsp?id=1595> (February 17, 2008).

6. Marian Mollin, "History 2004 Syllabus," *Virginia Tech Department of History*, n.d., <http://www.history.vt.edu/Mollin/2004syl.htm> (February 29, 2008).

7. Larry Magrid, "My Rules for Online Safety," *SafeKids.com*, n.d., <http://www.safekids.com/kidsrules.htm> (February 29, 2008).

8. University of St. Thomas Libraries, "How do you evaluate resources?" n.d., <http://www.stthomas.edu/libraries/research/tutorials/basic/evaluate.html> (March 3, 2008).

9. Nora Steiner Mealy, "Boinngg! Here come the armadillos," *Ranger Rick*, vol. 34, no. 11, November 2000, p. 13.

10. David Attenborough, *The Life of Mammals* (Princeton, N.J.: Princeton University Press, 2002), pp. 56–57.

11. Purdue University, "Writer's Block/Writer's Anxiety," *The OWL at Purdue*, n.d., <http://owl.english.purdue.edu/owl/resource/567/01/> (February 17, 2008).

12. CalTech University, "Tips for Peer Review," *Writing@Caltech*, n.d., <http://writing.caltech.edu/resources/peer-review-tips.html> (February 29, 2008).

Index